T0380231

Celebrate Military Kids!

Children's Songs, Rhymes & Chants, Craft ideas, Gym Class plans,
Story Time plans, Coloring Pages, Performance Plan, Instruments & Activities!

Laura Jo Ackerman

Get this 'Military Child, That's Me!' Classroom Set

Invest in a classroom set of books for your class.

You can find the music on Amazon, Apple Music, YouTube, Pandora, and more!

SPECIAL PAGES INCLUDED FOR YOU TO CREATE YOUR VERY OWN SCRAP BOOK!

Yes!

I am a Military Child

A book for Military Brats

A Song and Story by Laura Jo Ackerman

Illustrated by Dominique Gonzalez

Military Child That's Me!

Miss Laura & the Military Brats

Get your class T-shirts at 'Military Child That's Me!' on Etsy.

GATHER THESE RESOURCES AND LET'S GET STARTED!

MILITARY CHILD
THAT'S ME! MISS LAURA & THE MILITARY BRATS

Archway Publishing books may be ordered through booksellers or by contacting:

Archway Publishing
1663 Liberty Drive
Bloomington, IN 47403
www.archwaypublishing.com
844-669-3957

Because of the dynamic nature of the Internet, any web addresses or links contained in this book may have changed since publication and may no longer be valid. The views expressed in this work are solely those of the author and do not necessarily reflect the views of the publisher, and the publisher hereby disclaims any responsibility for them.

Any people depicted in stock imagery provided by Getty Images are models, and such images are being used for illustrative purposes only.
Certain stock imagery © Getty Images.

ISBN: 978-1-6657-4338-9 (sc)
ISBN: 978-1-6657-4337-2 (e)

Library of Congress Control Number: 2023908143

Print information available on the last page.

Archway Publishing rev. date: 11/06/2023

MILITARY CHILD
THAT'S ME!

Miss Laura &
the
Military Brats

Celebrate Military Kids!

April is the Month of the Military Child

During this month we pay tribute to military children for their commitment, sacrifice, and unconditional support for our troops.

Laura Jo Ackerman

Get this 'Military Child, That's Me!' Classroom Set

Invest in a classroom set of books for your class.

You can find the music on Amazon, Apple Music, YouTube, Pandora, and more!

SPECIAL PAGES INCLUDED FOR YOU TO CREATE YOUR VERY OWN SCRAP BOOK!

Get your class T-shirts at 'Military Child That's Me!' on Etsy.

Laura Jo Ackerman

@LorlaJo

MILITARY CHILD
THAT'S ME! MISS LAURA & THE MILITARY BRATS
Preschool/Elementary

The book is dedicated to all Military Brats, past, present, and future.

I would like to extend a special thank you to my husband for making his dream of traveling the world a reality by joining the Navy.

A very special thank you goes out to Jeffrey "Teddy" and Christopher, our two boys who made military life an adventure to remember. I couldn't have done it without you!

Thanks to the people who work in the libraries on U.S. Military Bases all around the world. In particular, Kevin Jones, Michelle Manfredi, and Anny Swanson. Our April celebrations were fun, celebratory, and full of learning about what it means to be a 'Brat'.

As I have gone through this process, I would like to thank my family for their support. It's taken time for 'Celebrate Military Kids!' to come about. Thank you for all your encouragement, support, editing, and suggestions.

This program's organizational style is inspired by Lynn Kleiner, an internationally renowned music educator and founder of Music Rhapsody. It was invaluable to have her encouragement. Lynn Kleiner's programs are excellent for those interested in teaching music and movement.

For her consultation during the creation of this material, I would like to thank Laurie Berkner.

Celebrate Military Kids!

by **Laura Ackerman**

CONTENTS

Celebrate Military Kids!

MILITARY CHILD, THAT'S ME!

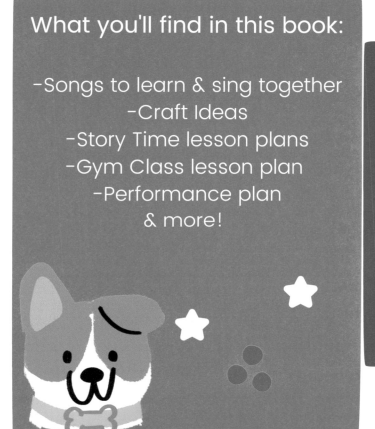

What you'll find in this book:

-Songs to learn & sing together
-Craft Ideas
-Story Time lesson plans
-Gym Class lesson plan
-Performance plan
& more!

Special activities that go along with the Month of the Military Child or Anytime.

Created by Laura Jo Ackerman
Based on her book
Yes! I Am a Military Child
and her music album
Miss Laura & the Military Brats

How to use this Program

- The *Celebrate Military Kids!* program was written for children from early childhood through about age 10. You are welcome to tweak the materials by changing the suggested story books, adding or editing suggested activities.

- *Yes! I Am a Military Child* was written for all military children. Many people who grew up as brats share this book with their own children to help them understand what being a military child is like.

- Children's military life experience is celebrated in this set in an all-encompassing way. Even though it does not say it, it is written with understanding and compassion for children who have lost a parent. Through this program, we nurture and acknowledge the loss of loved ones even when they are far away.

A note from Miss Laura:

- As a tribute to children who are military brats, I wrote the book *Yes! I Am A Military Child.* No matter where your life takes you, once you're a brat, you're a brat forever. You can face a lot of challenges when working with military brats. In times of disarray, the brat's teacher may be one of the only places where they feel safe. Your patience and kind heart will make this program a success!

Much love to you. Go have some fun!
-Miss Laura

Gather your crafting supplies
Shopping List:
Glue, scissors, tape, crayons & more

Boot Craft
- cardstock 81/2"x11", enough for 1/child
- hole puncher
- ribbon or lace cut 2'/child

Military Service Star Banner Craft
- large red paper 12"x14.5"
- smaller white paper 9"x12"
- yellow paper for fringe 2"x12"
- yellow yarn for hanging 20"
- blue stars, pattern included

Dandelion Craft
- white paper plate
- yellow construction paper 9"x12"
- white fluffy stuffing or cotton balls
- pinching style clothespin

Moving or PCS Craft
- large blue construction paper 12"x18"
- copies of images included
- a collection of real maps of America

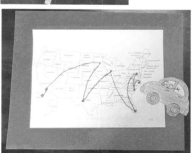

Windy Roads Craft
- large blue construction paper 12"x18"
- copies of images included
- a collection of real maps of America

Kick-Off Prep

Order your classroom supply of the book: 'Yes! I am a Military Child'.
- You should order enough books for each child to have one. As scrapbooks, each child will need their own book.
  - Order your supply of books on Amazon.com

Order your classroom suppply of T-shirts made and arrange for someone to sew superhero capes on.
- Pre-order t-shirts for distribution on your kick-off day.
  - Order T-shirts at www.Etsy.com/shop/militarychildthatsme
  - Ask a volunteer to sew on 12"x14" 'superhero' capes on the back. This is only a suggestions but please remember to not make them longer as they can cause an issue during a bathroom break!
  - About 12 capes can be made from 1 cut yard of fabric. Sew the edges of the capes with a serger or use a zig-zag stitch to keep it from fraying. You can also fold the edges over and sew, to hide the raw edge.

Download the album 'Military Child, That's Me!' so it is ready to play on opening day.
- Purchase the CD, download, or use your favorite streaming service
  - Amazon: https://tinyurl.com/4mx2uzp3
  - Spotify: https://open.spotify.com/album/1YNq3jUVT5hZNGhscoBMly
  - Pandora: https://www.pandora.com/artist/miss-laura-and-the-military-brats-childrens/military-child-thats-me/ALZkVj2mfhl9jJ2
  - YouTube: https://www.youtube.com/channel/UCYhxH5tl5VKg1XHuTMt4qVQ
  - Apple Music: https://music.apple.com/us/album/military-child-thats-me/1506852085

Shop for Crafting Supplies
- Gather crafting supplies.
  - Great places to shop for all your crafting needs:
    Hobby Lobby, Discount School Supply & Oriental Trading Co.

Get in touch with parents/caregivers as some project need input from them
- In some lesson plans, parents/caretakers will need to provide information for some projects.

Fitness Celebration
- Print fitness certificates, fill in and sign.
- Medals can be ordered from Crown Awards: www.crownawards.com

Resources

Books & Music
used in this program:

1. *A Paper Hug* Stephanie Skolmoski Illustrated by Anneliese Bennion
2. *Brave like Me* by Barbara Kerley
3. *My Daddy Sleeps Everywhere* Jesse Franklin, Illustrated by Tahna Desmond Fox
4. *Night Catch* Brenda Ehrmantraut, Illustrated by Vicki Wehrman
5. *Over There* Dorinda Silver Williams, LCSW-C, Illustrated by Branda Gilliam - There are two versions, a 'Daddy' version and a 'Mommy' version.
6. *The Berenstain Bears* Moving Day", Jan & Stan Berenstain
7. *While You Are Away* Eileen Spinelli, Illustrated by Renee Graef
8. *Yes! I am a Military Child* Laura Ackerman, Illustrated by Dominique Gonzalez

Further Resources

1. *Home Again* by Dorinda Silver Williams, Illustrated by Brenda Gilliam
2. *I'm Here For You Now* by Janice Im, Claire Lerner, Rebecca Parlakian, and Linda Eggbeer
3. *Momma's Boots* by Sandra Miller Linhart, Illustrated by Tahna Marie Desmond
4. *Daddy's Boots* by Sandra Miller Linhart, Illustrated by Tahna Marie Desmond
5. *Make Your Bed* by William H. McRaven, Illustrated by Howard McWilliam
6. *Yankee Doodle Mickey* by Disney
7. *Patriotic Kids' Songs* by Cooltime Kids
8. *Just Like The Sun* By The Laurie Berkner Band From Under A Shady Tree Album
9. *Veteran's Day PE Stations* 20 Military Movement Activity Cards at Teacherspayteachers.com
10. *Just Like the Sun* by The Laurie Berkner Band

CD Track Lisiting

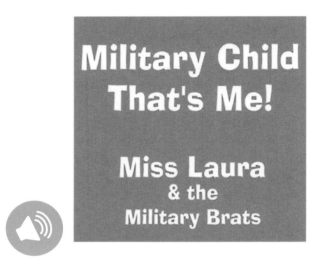

1. We're Military Brats
2. Military Child, That's Me!
3. Yes! I am a Military Child
4. Dandelion
5. The Pledge of Allegiance
6. The Star Spangled Banner
7. Windy, Windy Roads of America
8. Lullaby – Yes! I am a Military Child!
9. Bonus Track – Yes! I am a Military Child
10. Bonus Track – Windy, Windy Roads of America

Unit 1
We're Military Brats

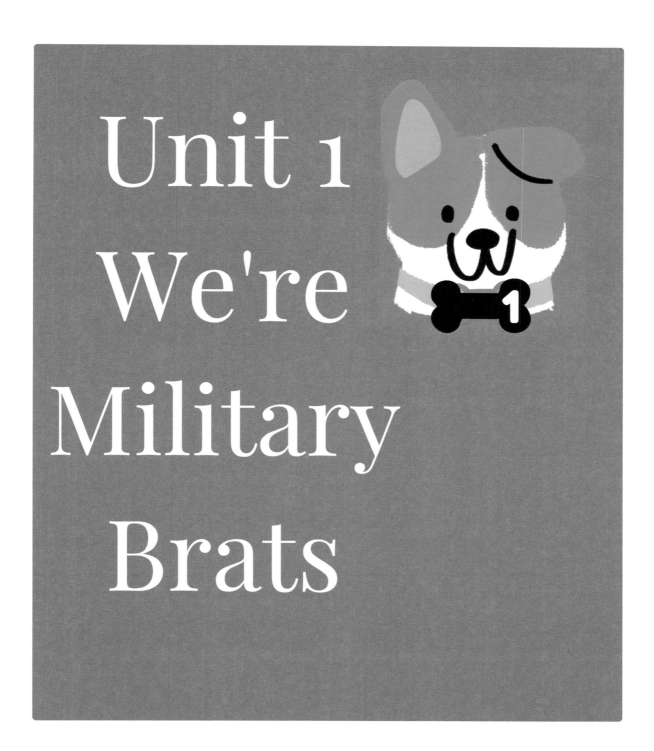

We're Military Brats

🔊 Track 1

An Echo & Chant song

Military Child That's Me!

Miss Laura & the Military Brats

Activity	Title	Tips for success	What's Needed
Listening Classroom entrance song	*Military Child, That's Me!*	Let children listen to the song. Sing the catchy chorus while tapping your knees.	*Track 2, by Miss Laura and the Military Brats*
Welcome Action Song	*If You're Ready for Story Time*	Throughout the program, the welcome song is repeated.	Class poster and lyrics included
Book	*Yes! I am a Military Child*	Introduce the children to the main theme book by reading the story. The children will each receive a book that has special pages for them to color and write in.	*by Laura Ackerman*
Activity	Everybody gets a book. *Yes! I am a Military Child*	The books should be handed out to the students. Each book should have their name on it. Teach them how to 'break it in' by opening the front and back and pressing open. Collect the book for later use after reading it together.	*by Laura Ackerman*
Book	*My Daddy Sleeps Everywhere*	There are many places where a servicemember might sleep while away from home.	*by Jesse Franklin and Tahna Desmond Fox*
Activity	*Wave the Flag*	To the tune of 'Row your Boat'	Scarves or American Flags - Class poster and lyrics included
Song	*We're Military Brats*	Listen to the song together.	*Track 1, by Miss Laura and the Military Brats*

We're Military Brats

 Track 1

An Echo & Chant song

Military Child That's Me!

Miss Laura & the Military Brats

Activity	Title	Tips for success	What's Needed
Activity	Discussion about being a Military Brat	Discuss being a Military Brat, and how you got to be one. (The word Brat today, is a good word. If you are talking about a little brat, you can refer to them as a Military Child.) Your life is different from many other children because one or both of your parents are serving or have served in the military. Kids who are brats are part of a club that spans the United States and beyond. To be a member of this club is a special experience. It is an honor to be referred to as a "Military Brat" and a "Military Child".	
Song	*We're Military Brats*	As the song becomes more familiar, pat legs and sing along. Children should echo your call and response. Create an exciting echo sound by splitting the room in two.	*Track 1, by Miss Laura and the Military Brats*
Book	*Home Again*	This is a story about preparing for the return of a service member.	*by Dorinda Silver Williams*
Goodbye Songs	*See you Later Alligator*	In the style of 'Clementine'	Class poster and lyrics included
Scrapbook Time	*Yes! I am a Military Child!*	Redistribute books. Turn to the first scrapbook page in the back of the book. Kids can draw pictures of themselves on this page. Friends who are brats can also be included. Make their scrapbook look nice by adding a background color of their choice.	*by Laura Ackerman*

We're Military Brats

 Track 1

An Echo & Chant song

We're Brats, we're Brats
We're Brats, we're Brats
We're Military Brats!

We're Brats, we're Brats
We're Brats, we're Brats
We're Military Brats!

I'm a Brat – I'm a Brat
You're a Brat – You're a Brat
He's a Brat – He's a Brat
She's a Brat – She's a Brat

We're Brats, we're Brats
We're Brats, we're Brats
We're Military Brats!

We're Brats, we're Brats
We're Brats, we're Brats
We're Military Brats

We're Brats, we're Brats
We're Brats, we're Brats
The Nicest Kind of Brats!

We're Brats, we're Brats
We're Brats, we're Brats
The Nicest Kind of Brats!

We're Brats, we're Brats
We're Brats, we're Brats
We're Military Brats!

We're Brats, we're Brats
We're Brats, we're Brats
We're Military Brats!

We're Military Brats

🔊 Track 1
An Echo & Chant song

Military Child That's Me!

Miss Laura & the Military Brats

Suggestions

Movement

- Listen to the chant with the students.
- Walk in place or around the room to the beat, chanting along to the music.
- Add marching feet to hear a strong beat.
- Add two quick claps after the word 'Brats' in the chorus part of the chant.
- Have a leader for the chant for the children to echo.
- Let the children share their ideas on what to do.

Performance

- Ask parents to allow their child to wear their work boots to march in for a fun effect.
- Have the children hold signs that say 'We're Brats' to hold up when they chant those words.
- You may want them to wear a t-shirt to identify what branch they represent.
- Make the children the callers and the audience the echo, being very very quiet at the beginning and quieting down at the end.

Instruments

- Add Tambourines to tap after the word 'brat' in the chorus.
- Add sticks to tap and keep the beat.

Unit 2
Military Child, That's Me!

Military Child, That's Me!

🔊 **Track 2**

Army, Navy Air Force, Marines
What do I have in my family?

Military Child That's Me!

Miss Laura
& the
Military Brats

Activity	Title	Tips for success	What's Needed
Listening Classroom entrance song	*Military Child, That's Me!*	Follow the movement suggestions in the song and sing and use the new actions.	**Track 2, by *Miss Laura and the Military Brats*** 🔊
Welcome Action Song	*If You're Ready for Story Time*	Throughout the program, the welcome song is repeated.	Class poster and lyrics included
Book	***Yes! I am a Military Child***	Read the story from lesson one.	*by Laura Ackerman*
Activity	***Yes! I am a Military Child***	Read and sing the recorded song, Track 3 on the album, again.	*by Laura Ackerman*
Book	*Night Catch*	"When a soldier's work takes him half-way around the world, he enlists the help of the North Star for a nightly game of catch with his son."	*by Brenda Ehrmantraut*
Song	***Dandelion***	Read the chant to the children. Listen to the recording and sing along.	***Track 4, by Miss Laura and the Military Brats*** 🔊
Activity	*Wave the Flag*	To the tune of 'Row your Boat'	Scarves or American Flags – Class poster and lyrics included
Activity	*Down at the Flag Pole*	To the tune of 'Down by the Station'	Scarves, American flags or make patriotic ribbon rings

Military Child, That's Me!

 Track 2

Army, Navy Air Force, Marines
What do I have in my family?

Military Child That's Me!

Miss Laura & the Military Brats

Activity	Title	Tips for success	What's Needed
Song	*We're Military Brats*	As the song becomes more familiar, pat legs and sing along. Children should echo your call and response. Split the class in half to create an exciting echo effect.	*Track 1, by Miss Laura and the Military Brats*
Goodbye Songs	*See you Later Alligator*	The goodbye song is repeated throughout the program.	Class poster and lyrics included
Scrapbook Time	*Yes! I am a Military Child*	Redistribute books. Turn to the second scrapbook page in the back of the book. Kids can draw pictures of their family on this page. Make their scrapbook look nice by adding a background color of their choice.	*by Laura Ackerman*
Coloring Book!	Military Coloring Pages / packets	The coloring packets should be made for each student. Simply copy and assemble the included images at the back of this book.	Crayons/ Markers

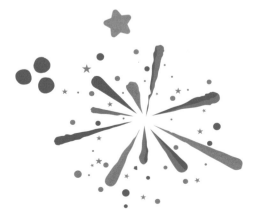

Military Child, That's Me!

🔊 Track 2

Army, Navy Air Force, Marines
What do I have in my family?

Military Child, That's Me!

Chorus

by Laura Ackerman

Mil i tar y Child, that's Me! Mil i tar y child,

that's me. Mil i tar y child, that's

me. I've got Mil i tar y in my fam i ly.

Chorus

Military Child, that's me! Military Child, that's me!
Military Child, that's me! I've got Military in my family.

Army!

Spoken: In the Army, they have Tanks and they can drive just about anywhere!
The Army drives big tanks,
the Army drives big tanks.
The Army drives big tanks,
for the United States of America!

Navy!

Spoken: In the Navy, they have Big, gray ships. They sail them all around the waters of the world!
The Navy sails big ships,
the Navy sails big ships.
The Navy sails big ships,
for the United States of America!

Air Force!

*Spoken: The Air Force has what? AIRPLANES! JETS!
Way high up in the sky!*
The Air Force flies big jets,
the Air Force flies big jets.
The Air Force flies big jets,
for the United States of America!

Marines!

Spoken: Marines are always ready. They are ready to go faster than you can say GO!
Marines are always ready, Marines are always ready.
Marines are always ready,
for the United States of America!
Chorus

Military Child, That's Me!

🔊 Track 2

Army, Navy Air Force, Marines
What do I have in my family?

Military Child
That's Me!

Miss Laura
& the
Military Brats

Suggestions

Movement
- Listen and sing together.
- Practice shouting out Army! Navy! Air Force! Marines!
- Add hand movements. Outstretched arms with thumbs up for 'Military Child'. Bring thumbs in and point to self and sing 'That's Me!' For 'I have Military in my Family' - make a big circle with the arms.
- Army! Drive a Tank, hold a pretend steering wheel and move around the room.
- Navy! Steer a Ship, pretend to hold a ship's wheel, or use a hula-hoop and spin and turn, moving the body side to side.
- Air Force! Stretch out arms turning the body into an airplane and move around the room flying far and wide.
- Marines! Go from a wobbly position into a 'stand at attention' stance. Touch your heels together looking 'ready'!

Performance
- For performance create a large poster picture (or two or three) of a tank, a ship, an airplane and a Marine at attention. As the verses are sung, child walks each large picture across the stage, moving it side to side to the beat.
- With children wearing the Miss Laura's 'Military Child That's Me!' red t-shirt, point to 'That's Me!' on the shirt singing it in the song.
- Give the children and opportunity to represent their family branch of the military by wearing an Army, Navy, Air Force or Marines t-shirt.
- Group kids by branch and sing their part when in the song. Someone in the group can hold a sign that shows who they are representing.
- Encourage the audience to sing the last chorus with the kids.

Instruments/Movement
- Children tap sticks in the quiet beat after each time 'Military Child' is sung.
- Make patriotic ribbon rings out of crepe paper for the children to wave over head when 'for the United States of America' is sung.

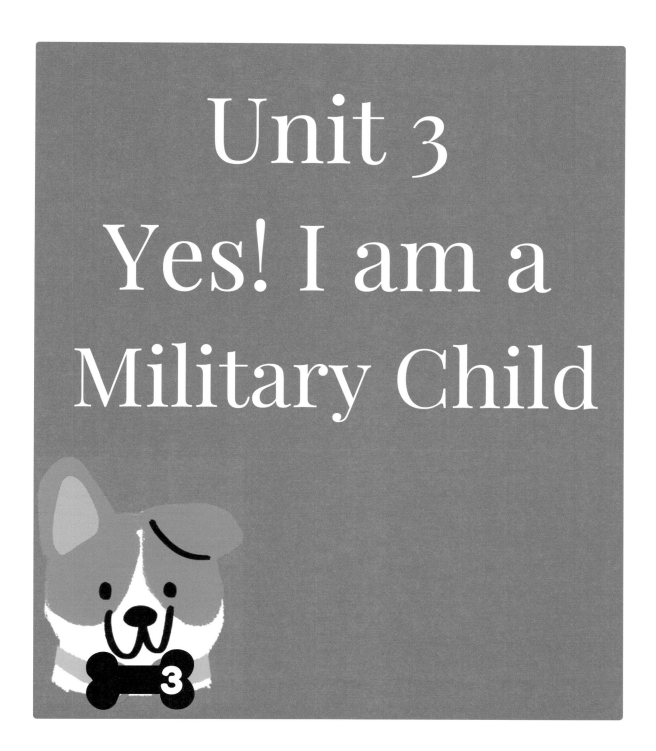

Unit 3
Yes! I am a Military Child

Yes! I am a Military Child

🔊 Track 3

Sometimes my life is really, Really WILD!

Military Child That's Me!

Miss Laura
& the
Military Brats

Activity	Title	Tips for success	What's Needed
Listening Classroom entrance song	**We're Military Brats**	Listen, pat legs and sing along while the song becomes more familiar. Have children echo your call and response. Split the room in two to have an exciting echo sound.	**Track 1, by Miss Laura and the Military Brats**
Welcome Action Song	*If You're Ready for Story Time*	The welcome song is repeated throughout the program.	Class poster and lyrics included
Activity	*Did you ever Raise a Flag?*	Add actions of 'moving this way and that way'.	Scarves – Class poster and lyrics included
Book	*The Berenstain Bears' Moving Day*	Follow Mama, Papa, and Brother as they pack up, say goodbye to friends, and move from the mountains down a sunny dirt road.	*by Jan and Stan Berenstain*
Song	**Windy, Windy Roads of America**	Take a listen and sing along. It's a tune that takes you and your family from one home to the next, military style.	**Track 7 by Miss Laura and the Military Brats**
Book	*A Paper Hug*	It's a sweet book about sending hugs along when your parent goes somewhere else. Make a paper hug part of your crafting plans.	*by Stephanie Skolmoski*
Activity	*Did you ever Wave a Flag*	To the tune of 'Did you ever see a Lassie?'	Scarves or American Flags – Class poster and lyrics included

Yes! I am a Military Child

 Track 3

Sometimes my life is really, Really WILD!

Military Child That's Me!

Miss Laura
& the Military Brats

Activity	Title	Tips for success	What's Needed
Activity	*Down at the Flag Pole*	To the tune of 'Down by the Station'	Scarves, American Flags or make patriotic ribbon rings. – Class poster and lyrics included
Song	**Yes! I am a Military Child**	This is a soft melody of a lullaby. While listening, children hold something soft to rock.	**Track 9, by Miss Laura and the Military Brats**
Goodbye Songs	*See you Later Alligator*	The goodbye song is repeated throughout the program.	Class poster and lyrics included
Scrapbook Time	**Yes! I am a Military Child**	Redistribute books. Turn to the third scrapbook page in the back of the book. Children draw or attach pictures of places they have been and or lived. Make their scrapbook look nice by adding a background color of their choice.	**by Laura Ackerman**

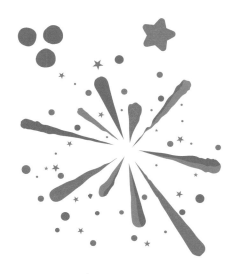

Yes! I am a Military Child

Track 3

Sometimes my life is really, Really WILD!

Military Child That's Me!

Miss Laura
& the
Military Brats

Yes! I am a Military Child

by Laura Ackerman

Yes! I am a mil i tar y child Some

times my life is real ly, real ly wild! My

Fam il ly sticks to- gether like glue with

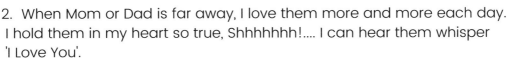

hugs and kiss es and gigg les

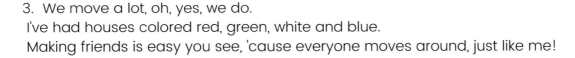

too!

2. When Mom or Dad is far away, I love them more and more each day.
I hold them in my heart so true, Shhhhhhh!.... I can hear them whisper
'I Love You'.

3. We move a lot, oh, yes, we do.
I've had houses colored red, green, white and blue.
Making friends is easy you see, 'cause everyone moves around, just like me!

4. My mom and dad are really strong, this military life can seem so long.
But in the end, this much is true: My family sticks together,
My family sticks together, My family sticks together, Just like glue!

Yes! I am a Military Child

🔊 Track 3

Sometimes my life is really, Really WILD!

Military Child That's Me!

Miss Laura
& the
Military Brats

Suggestions

Movement & Performance
- Listen and sing together
- Add actions
1. Nod for 'Yes'
2. Show hands as tiger claws for 'wild'
3. Cross arms in front for 'hugs'
4. Place hand over eyes for 'far away'
5. Pat heart for 'Love them'
6. Place finger in front of mouth for 'shhhh!'
7. Smile and wave at neighbor for 'making friends'
8. Show muscle arms for 'really strong'.
9. Clap hands and hold for each 'stick together'.
10. Hold hands still together through 'just like glue'.

Instruments
- Children tap sticks in the quiet beat after each phrase. 'Yes! I am a military child, TAP, sometimes my life is really, really, wild, TAP', etc.

Unit 4
Dandelion

Dandelion

🔊 Track 4

The Flower of the Military Child

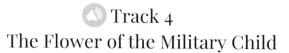

Miss Laura
& the
Military Brats

Activity	Title	Tips for success	What's Needed
Listening Classroom entrance song	**Windy, Windy Roads of America**	With the music, children dance, sing, and groove!	*Track 10, by Miss Laura and the Military Brats* 🔊
Welcome Action Song	*If You're Ready for Story Time*	The welcome song is repeated throughout the program.	Class poster and lyrics included
Book	*Brave Like Me*	Here's a story about how even kids need to be brave.	*by Barbara Kerley*
Song	**Dandelion**	The tune shows military kids how they grow and fly, just like a dandelion flower.	*Track 4, by Miss Laura and the Military Brats* 🔊
Activity	*Did you ever raise a Flag?*	To the tune of 'Did you ever see a Lassie?'	Class poster and lyrics included
Book	*While You Are Away*	Children will learn how others stay close to their family members even though they are far away from them.	*by Eileen Spinelli*
Activity	**The Pledge of Allegiance**	Talking points: • Flags represent countries • Flags have many meanings • Why we have stars and stripes • Explain that countries have a pledge to their flag almost the same as ours!	*Track 5, by Miss Laura and the Military Brats* 🔊

Dandelion

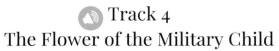

🔊 Track 4
The Flower of the Military Child

Military Child That's Me!

Miss Laura
& the
Military Brats

Activity	Title	Tips for success	What's Needed
Activity	*Down at the Flag Pole*	To the tune of 'Down by the Station'	Scarves, American Flags or make patriotic ribbon rings. – Class poster and lyrics included
Song	**We're Military Brats**	Check out this marching tune and refresh your memory.	**Track 1, by Miss Laura and the Military Brats** 🔊
Goodbye Songs	*See you Later Alligator*	The goodbye song is repeated throughout the program.	Class poster and lyrics included
Scrapbook Time	**Yes! I am a Military Child**	Distribute books. Turn to the third scrapbook page in the back of the book. Go to the Tell a Story page. Children can write or draw a story about a family travel adventure they had.	**by Laura Ackerman**

Dandelion

by Laura Ackerman

I will grow an-y where. I'll see the world here and there. I'll make new friends it's ea-sy you'll see 'cause every-body moves a round just like Me!

Dandelions, the flower of the military child. Military children bloom everywhere the winds carry them. They are hearty and upright, their roots are strong, cultivated deeply in the culture of the military, planted swiftly and surely.

1. I will grow anywhere, I'll see the world here and there.
I'll make new friends its easy you'll see, this military life just can't be beat

2. Dandelion, Dandelion, growing in the ground. Your yellow flower is big and round.
Do you know you're just like me? A little child in the Military

3. I will grow anywhere, I'll see the world here and there.
I'll make new friends its easy you'll see, This military life just can't be beat.

4. Dandelion, Dandelion, growing in the ground. Your puffy flower is white and round.
Big winds blow, your seeds sail away, I know we'll meet again in a place far away!

5. I will grow anywhere, I'll see the world here and there.
I'll make new friends its easy you'll see. This military life just can't be beat.

Dandelion

🔊 Track 4
The Flower of the Military Child

Military Child That's Me!

Miss Laura
& the
Military Brats

Suggestions

Movement & Performance Suggestions
- Listen and sing together.
- Clap along.
- Practice the chant quietly, standing with hands on knees, bouncing to the beat.
- Wave hands above the head when singing, 'I will go anywhere'.
- Add creative movements singing 'here and there', etc.
- You can make the Dandelion craft by following the instructions. You can use it while singing the song. There is a yellow side for the yellow dandelion and a white side for the puffy flower. You'll have a beautiful field of flowers if you wave them high. Add green streamers for a festive and eye-catching effect.

Instruments
- Children tap rhythm sticks in place of hand clapping.
- Play a triangle sound at the end of each phrase when it is quiet. The quiet occurs after 'ground', 'round', 'me?' & 'military'. In the second part, after 'ground', 'round', 'blow', 'away', and the last 'away'.
- Introduce stamping and clapping alternately. Stomp on 'dan' and clap on 'lion'.

Unit 5
Windy, Windy Roads of America

Windy, Windy Roads of America

🔊 Track 7

How we move when it's time.

Activity	Title	Tips for success	What's Needed
Listening Classroom entrance song	**Military Child, That's Me! The Star Spangled Banner The Pledge of Allegiance**	Sing along, recite the Pledge, and learn the National Anthem.	**Tracks 2, 5 & 6 by Miss Laura and the Military Brats** 🔊
Welcome Action Song	*If You're Ready for Story Time*	The welcome song is repeated throughout the program.	Class poster and lyrics included
Song	*Did you ever raise a flag?*	Add actions of 'moving this way and that way'.	Small American Flags – Class poster and lyrics included
Activity	*Wave the Flag*	To the tune of 'Row your Boat'	Scarves or American Flags – Class poster and lyrics included
Book	**Yes! I am A Military Child**	At this point, the children should know it very well.	**by Laura Ackerman**
Song	**The Star Spangled Banner**	Spend a few minutes discussing the national anthem. Don't forget to sing it! Someone should hold an American flag. Then you can talk about 'Colors' and 'Taps'.	**Track 6 by Miss Laura and the Military Brats** 🔊
Book	*Over There*	A book to remind children their deployed parent loves and cares about them every day.	*by Dorinda Silver Williams, LCSW-C*

Windy, Windy Roads of America

🔊 Track 7

How we move when it's time.

Activity	Title	Tips for success	What's Needed
Activity	*Performance run through*	Collect props and run through songs and actions for the end of the week/month show. Run through the songs with the crafted artwork, instruments, and actions.	
Goodbye Songs	*See you Later Alligator*	The goodbye song is repeated through the program.	Class poster and lyrics included
Scrapbook Time	**Yes! I am a Military Child**	Distribute books. Turn to the fifth scrapbook page in the back of the book. Children draw or attach photos of their military family members. The kids can draw whatever they like on the Free Page at the end.	

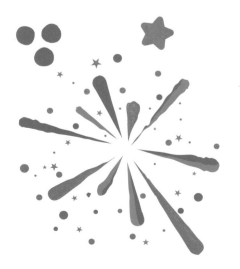

Windy, Windy Roads of America

 Track 7

How we move when it's time.

Windy, Windy Roads of America

by Laura Ackerman

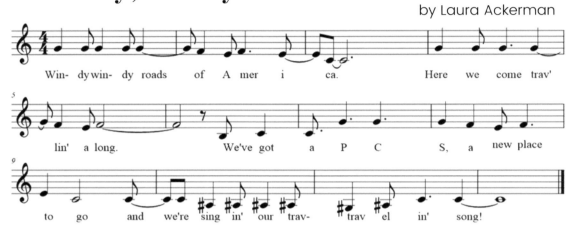

Win- dy win- dy roads of A mer i ca. Here we come trav'-

lin' a long. We've got a P C S, a new place

to go and we're sing in' our trav- trav el in' song!

Chorus:
Windy, windy roads of America,
here we come travelling along,
We've got a P-C-S, a new place to go,
and we're singing our travelling song!
Windy, windy roads of America,
here we come travelling along.
There's a new place that's going to be
our home and it's time to get moving
along.

1. Three years or so is when we go,
most military kids do.
Across the state or the USA,
or over an ocean or two!

Chorus

2. We've got Army and Navy kids to
meet, Marine and Air Force, too.
Some from the Coast Guard and DoD,
all moving someplace new!

Chorus
Movers come with their big trucks,
boxes and tape galore.
The job is big, they get it done,
faster than any chore!
Toys? Packed! Beds? Packed! Bikes?
Packed! Teddy Bears? Packed!
The dog? The Dog? THE DOG?
In the kennel and ready to go!

Chorus

3. Sometimes it's hard to say goodbye,
to friends you know so well.
sometimes you just gotta cry and cry...
so go ahead. Let it all out.
We're all in this together. We are.

Chorus

Windy, Windy Roads of America

🔊 Track 7
How we move when it's time.

Suggestions

Talking Points

- Take a moment to listen to the song and talk about what it says.
- Can you tell me what these kids are doing? How will they get there?
- Are they scared? How do all their things get to a new house?
- How does the dog get there?
- Did they almost forget the dog?
- Do you think they cried when it was time to go?
- Is it possible that they cried several times?
- What did they see at their new place?
- Was there a pool there? Did they go swimming?
- Have they met any new kids who might become friends with them?
- How did you get to where we are now? A plane? a train? a bus? a car?

Military
Kids
Gym
Class

Adding Fitness to your Celebration is Easy!

This section includes a lesson plan you can use for your classes.

Things to include in your fitness event:

- Running Races
- Push-ups station
- Sit-ups station
- Tug-of-War
- Parachute play
- Military theme relay races
- Measure height
- Award certificates
- Medals

Military Kids Gym Class

Little Military Athletes
Little Military Fitness Test

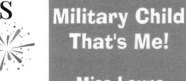

Military Child That's Me!

Miss Laura & the **Military Brats**

Activity	Tips for Success	What's Needed
1. Warm-Up	Provide each child with an instrument for the military marching band. It is suggested that you use tambourines, shakers, triangles, drums, or other instruments.	Disney's ***Yankee Doodle Mickey***
2. Hula Hoop free time and group game	Make sure there are enough hula hoops for everyone. One peppy song should be allowed free play. • I like Disney's *Encanto* Group hooping activity: '*Just Like the Sun*' Demonstrate what the sun does in the song. For example: 1. Sun is up – hoop is up 2. Sun is down – hoop goes down and 3. Children go inside to 'sleep' 4. Sun is up/cloudy day – 'hide' hoop behind you/you are a big cloud 5. Sun is up- hoop is up.	Class supply of hula hoops Your choice of Music Suggested: *Columbia, mi Encanto*, Disney *Just Like the Sun*, by The Laurie Berkner Band
3. Stretching	Stretch gently to warm up. Make sure you stretch tall and small. Get your arms and legs out and tip them from side to side. Make the body twist by touching the toes, standing, and touching the toes. Make poses with the 'Air Craft Carrier Shooter' images included in this book!	Shooter image included in this book Patriotic Music
4. Running	Military kids may feel the need to 'go crazy' to the music. Make it fun and fast! I suggest using Billy Joel's *Rootbeer Rag* After running, begin races from one side of the room to the other. Start with a magic word like "On your mark, get set, go aaaaaand... PEANUT BUTTER!"	The program t-shirts with super-hero capes work perfectly with this part of the class. If you want, make or buy capes. You can find them at www.OrientalTrading.com **Track 7 – *Windy, Windy Roads of America*** and other peppy music.

Military Kids Gym Class

Little Military Athletes
Little Military Fit Test

Military Child That's Me!

Miss Laura
& the
Military Brats

Activity	Tips for Success	What's Needed
5. Military 'Physical Readiness Test' Activities	Review the poses for the 'Aircraft Carrier Shooter'. Do jumping jacks, push-ups, and sit-ups together. It is common for military personnel to be measured. Measure their height, tell them the number, and tell them something positive. For example: *You are a great learner. You are growing strong. You are a good friend. You are kind. You make a difference. You are capable. You are creative. You can do hard things.* The kids will respond with smiles!	'Shooter' picture, Measuring tape Your choice of Music
6. Circle Time	Make sure everyone drinks water before circle time. Get together in a circle or group. Sing and clap along to 'Dandelion'. Introduce 'The Peanut Song'. At the end of this book, it is included with the songs.	**Track 4. *Dandelion* *The Peanut Song***
7. Celebratory Activity	Get the parachute out for some fun and engaging games. Sing this song or chant to help the children follow directions: • *And shake and shake and shake and shake and shake and shake and Stop!* Sing four times. Children enjoy being praised for following directions and listening well. Shake the chute with some music, add some balls, and play some games.	Classroom size parachute & Your choice of peppy music
8. Closing Marching Band	You can play new patriotic songs or classroom favorites.	Instruments & Music Your choice of Music
9. Final Stretch	Gather in a circle. Play the lullaby version of ***Yes! I am a Military Child***. Let the children stretch and discuss what they accomplished today. We are proud of what we have accomplished.	***Track 8*** ***Lullaby - Yes! I am a Military Child***
10. Awards Ceremony	The certificate of completion included at the end of this book should be presented to each child. If you chose medals, plan a medal ceremony. The accomplishment of modeling a parent's fitness test is exciting.	Signed and Dated Certificates for each participant

You can incorporate these poses into your gym class warm-ups and running races.

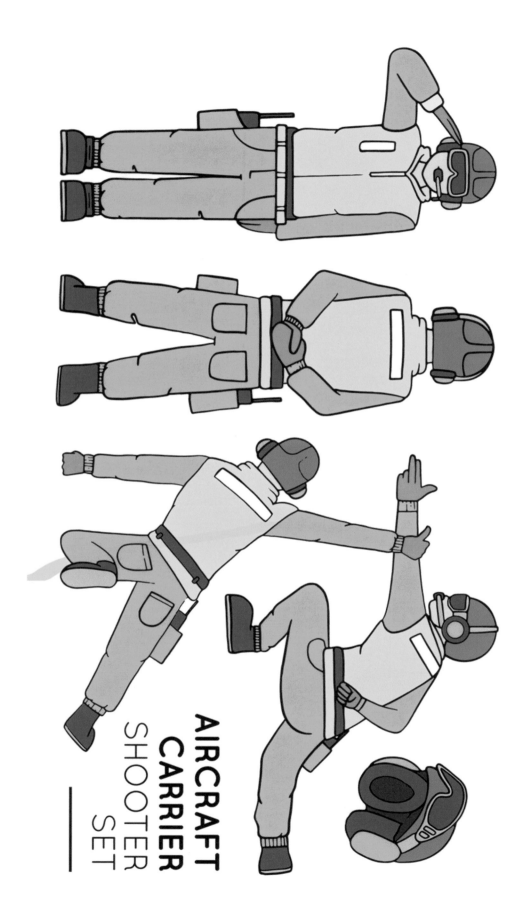

AIRCRAFT CARRIER
SHOOTER SET

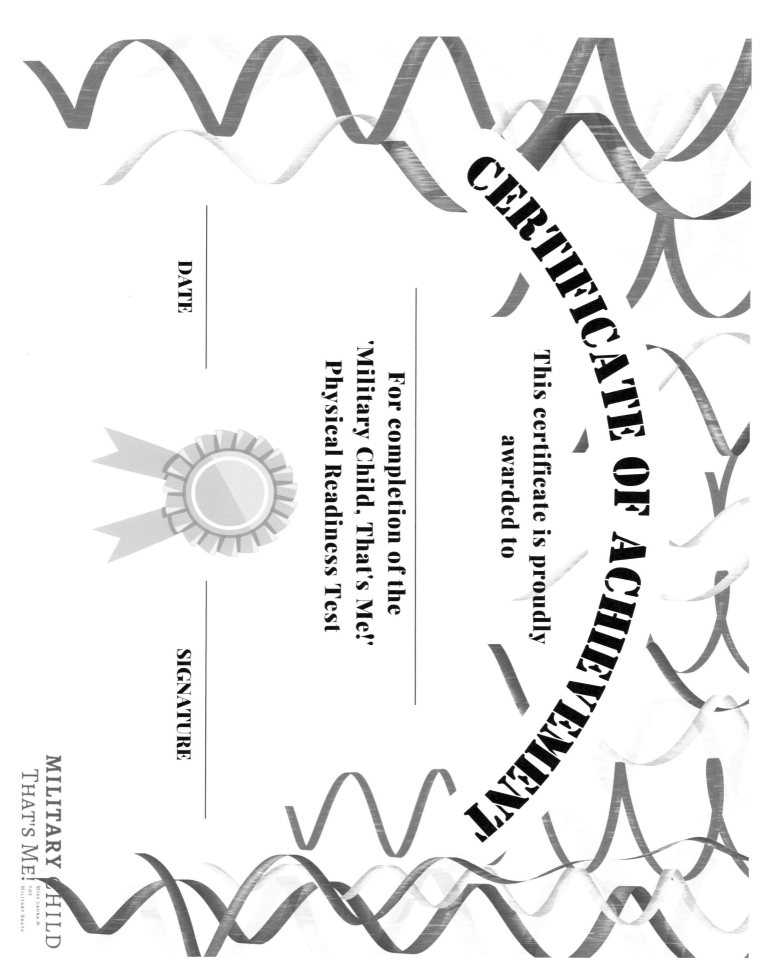

CERTIFICATE OF ACHIEVEMENT

This certificate is proudly awarded to

For completion of the
'Military Child, That's Me!'
Physical Readiness Test

DATE

SIGNATURE

MILITARY CHILD
THAT'S ME! MISS LAURA &
THE MILITARY BRATS

41

Sing Along Songs

Down at the Flagpole
Tune: Down by the Station

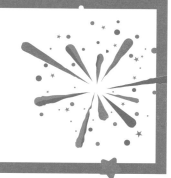

Down at the flagpole,
Early in the morning,
We will raise our flag,
The red, white, and blue.
We stand at attention,
It's something that we do.
We salute the colors,
The red, white, and blue.

Wave the Flag
Tune: Row your Boat

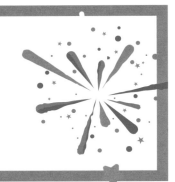

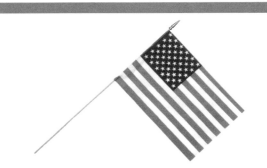

Wave, wave, wave the flag,
Hold it very high.
Watch the colors gently wave,
Way up in the sky.

March, march, march around,
Hold the flag up high.
Wave, wave, wave the flag,
Way up in the sky.

Did you ever Wave a Flag?
Tune: Did you ever See a Lassie

Did you ever wave a flag?
A flag, a flag?
Did you ever wave a flag?
Up in the sky?
Wave this way and that way,
And this way and that way.
Did you ever wave a flag
Up in the sky?

Hello Song
Tune: If You're Happy

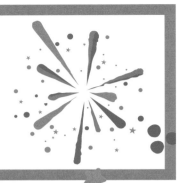

If you're ready for a story, clap your hands!
If you're ready for a story, clap your hands!
If you're ready for a story,
If you're ready for a story,
If you're ready for a story, clap your hands!
(Nod your head, rub your tummy, sit so still)

The Peanut Song

Traditional

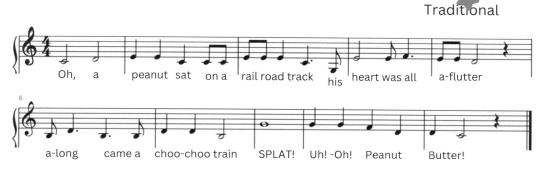

Oh, a Peanut sat
on a railroad track
His heart was
all a-flutter
along came a
choo-choo train
Splat!
Uh-Oh Peanut Butter!

Bring in a train whistle, and blow it to start the song. Teach the song and have fun!

Goodbye Song
Tune: Clementine

See you later, alligator,
In a while, crocodile,
Give a hug, lady bug,
Blow a kiss, jelly fish.
See you soon, big baboon,
Out the door, dinosaur,
Take care, polar bear,
Wave goodbye, butterfly.

Crafts

We're Military Brats

🔊 **Track 1**
An Echo & Chant song

Military Child That's Me!

Miss Laura
& the
Military Brats

Military Boot Craft

What you need:

1. beige cardstock 81/2"x11"
2. scissors
3. crayons
4. hole puncher
5. ribbon or lace cut 2'/child
6. tape may be needed for your choice of lace or ribbon

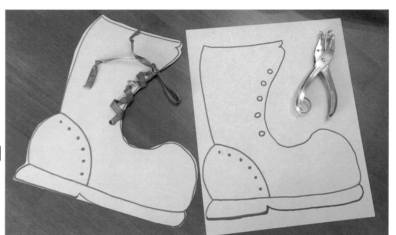

How to do it:

- Photocopy the included image onto plain or colored cardstock. If plain, the children can color the boot.
- Cut out and punch holes where the laces will go.
- Cut a ribbon or use a shoelace to 'lace' up the boot. If using ribbon, knot or tape the ends for easier lacing for little fingers.
- Leave enough lace at the top of the boot for tying and lace through the holes from top to bottom and back to the top again. Tie as you like.
- You may want to add the child's picture or name to the boot or ask them how they would like to finish it.

MILITARY CHILD
THAT'S ME! Miss Laura & THE Military Brats

Military Child, That's Me!

Military Child That's Me!

Miss Laura
& the
Military Brats

Military Service Star Banner Craft

What you need:

1. large red paper 12"x14.5"
2. smaller white paper 9"x12"
3. yellow paper for fringe 2"x12"
4. yellow yarn for hanging 20"
5. hole punch
6. blue stars, pattern included
7. glue
8. scissors
9. tape

How to do it:

- Assemble the crafts as shown, centering and gluing the white paper on top of the red paper.
- Cut out and glue on the needed number of stars.
- Reinforce top corners with tape and punch holes for string.
- Cut and tie the string to the red paper
- Cut fringes on the yellow paper and glue to the bottom back of the red paper.
- Hang and display.

MILITARY CHILD
THAT'S ME! Miss Laura &
THE
Military Brats

Yes! I am a Military Child

🔊 **Track 3**
Sometimes my life is really, Really WILD!

Military Child That's Me!

Miss Laura
& the
Military Brats

Moving or PCS Craft

What you need:

1. large blue construction paper
2. copies of images included
3. a collection of real maps of America
4. glue
5. scissors

How to do it:

- Have all pieces cut and ready for the craft, including the map section.
- Glue map on first, then the border phrases. PCS can go anywhere the child likes.
- The two houses they select should be on the left and right of the page.
- Consider using an **exacto** knife to 'cut open' the doors of the van so they can somewhat open and close over the furniture the child chooses to pack in the van.

PCS
We Move a lot, Oh, Yes, We Do!

Dandelion

 Track 4
The Flower of the Military Child

Dandelion Craft

What you need:

1. white paper plate
2. yellow construction paper 9"x12"
3. white fluffy stuffing or cotton balls
4. pinching style clothespin
5. glue
6. scissors

How to do it:

- Trace the paper plate onto the yellow paper.
- Cut out the yellow circle. You may also cut 2-3" cuts around to give it more of a dandelion flower look
- You may want to give the edges of the yellow a curled up look by rolling it gently around a pencil
- Apply glue to the back of the yellow and center on the paper plate.
- Turn the plate over and apply small amounts of glue, enough to hold small fluffs of cotton balls or white fluffy stuffing.
- Clip on the clothespin and let dry.

Use with the fun **Dandelion** song!

Windy, Windy Roads of America

🔊 Track 7

How we move when it's time.

Windy Roads Craft

What you need:

1. a map of the US for each child
2. large colored paper to mount the map upon
3. car cut out
4. crayons
5. scissors

What to do:

- Show an image of the United States of America.
- Place on the map where your base is and others, too.
- Have the children do the same by asking their parents ahead of time for info. Or, just place dots on the map.
- Connect the dots with a crayon or marker.
- Talk about up and down on the map and side to side. Talk about north, south, east, west.
- How do their dots go? Can they trace them with their finger.
- Have the children cut out and color their car.
- As you listen and sing the song, have the children 'drive' their car around during the choruses.

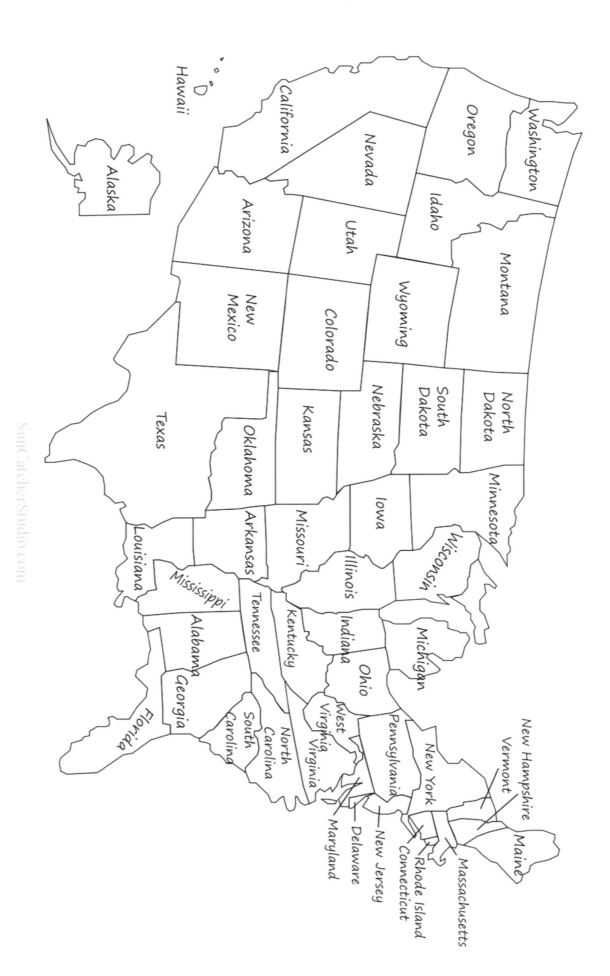

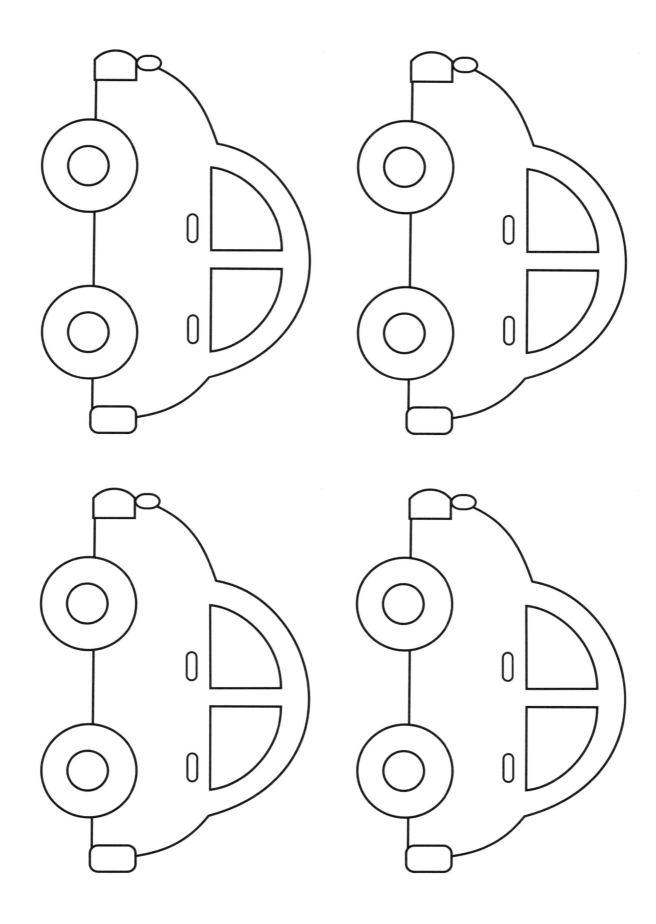

Military Child, That's Me!

🔊 Track 2

Army, Navy Air Force, Marines

What do I have in my family?

Coloring Pages

Marines

Coast Guard

Air Force

Air Force

U.S. AIR FORCE FU-122

Air Force

Performance Planner

Concert Date_____ Time _____ Location _____

TO DO FIRST

- Plan a location, multipurpose space, gym, cafeteria, and a space large enough to hold kids and guests as soon as possible.

- Parents should also be informed of the concert date as early as possible. Share it on social media.

- Publish dates on the school calendar, send home reminders, post signs in classrooms, at entrances, etc.

- Consider the length of your program. There should be roughly 30 minutes in a preschool program and 45 minutes in an elementary program.

TASK LIST

- Decide who will be the MC for the show. MCs introduce the groups and lead the program. Keep the event flowing by asking the MC to share light tidbits about military life.
- You might want to invite a color guard or arrange for children to carry the American flag and all branches of the service flags. If you are based in a foreign country, include the flag of that country.
- To begin the program, recite the Pledge of Allegiance and sing the Notional Anthem.
- Prepare a program guide that greeters can distribute. I have provided an example.

NOTES

Before the event, ask parents to dress everyone in red, white, and blue. 'Military Child, That's Me!' shirts can be worn also.

As guests enter, play festive and patriotic music, including 'Yankee Doodle Mickey' or 'Patriotic Kids' Songs' by Cooltime Kids

- Choose guest speakers. Ask them to give a short talk about their experiences as a service member, spouse, or caregiver

- Stay in touch as the event approaches. You don't want to lose your speakers due to poor communication.

Performance Planner

Concert Date_____ Time _____ Location _____

PERFORMANCE START SUGGESTIONS

1. Welcome all guests with a grand and uplifting message.

As an example:

"Welcome parents, grandparents, caregivers, family and friends. We are thankful that we can gather today to celebrate our children of the US Military. For those who cannot be with us today, we hold them close to our hearts at this time. (Let there be a little silence here.)

We are excited for the children to share what they have learned over the course of our time with this special theme, 'Yes! I am a Military Child'. We are happy you are here to join us for this very special celebration as you sit back, relax, and enjoy this very special day. We are so proud of the kids and their teachers and look forward to seeing them perform."

2. Lights! Camera! Action!

Silence the audience by dimming or turning off a few lights. Turn up the lights as the children march in.

'We're Military Brats' chant.

Quietly, the children are at the entrances.
Begin the program with the children stomping into the room chanting "We're Military Brats" using the recording from 'Miss Laura & the Military Brats'. The teachers lead the children to their space for the remainder of the performance. Children may sit or stand.

3. Get creative!

In the event that a color guard is present, have them enter after all the children are present. You can have children carry the flags in and stand in front if you do not have a color guard.

The National Anthem and Pledge of Allegiance should be sung once everyone is in their places. You should also play the anthem of the foreign country if you're there.

Stage Presence:

Put tape on the floor to indicate where each class should be. You might consider putting an 'x' to mark where children stand.

Each group should use a special prop. A dandelion craft is used in the song 'Dandelion'. Each group should use its own musical instrument For example, the younger kids have shakers while the older kids have tambourines or triangles.

Each group now sings a Military or Patriotic song and songs from Miss Laura & the Military Brats, ending with full group participation for the last song. The audience joins in as well. The speaker thanks parents for their service and acknowledges them It's time for a memorable treat!

Celebrate Military Kids!

Ideas to make your celebration of Military Kids Incredibly Awesome!

Where is the World Wall

- Bulletin board or wall mural of world
- Children can place a dot where they have been and where they have family & friends

What Time is it?

- Use the 'Where in the World Wall' to talk about time changes
- Discuss who is sleeping now?

Purple Up for Military Kids!

- Purple Day!
- Purple Crafts
- Sing *We're Military Brats*
- Sing *Yes! I am a Military Child*
- Mix colors red & blue

'Where I am From' writing or picture drawing activity

- Children write a story/draw about where they are from.
- Share the stories daily

Poster Contest

- Do a coloring page from the collection in this book
- Create your own military themed art
- Ribbons
- Create an art room for visiting parents

Favorite Service Day

- Sing *Military Child, That's Me!*
- Discuss favorite branches
- Tell why they are a favorite

Announce interesting military-kid facts each day.

Host a breakfast or assembly with older military kids as guest speakers.

THANK YOU
FOR SERVING,
PROTECTING, AND
KEEPING AMERICA
SAFE.

MILITARY CHILD
THAT'S ME!

PRESENTING
MILITARY
CHILD,
THAT'S ME!

79

CELEBRATE MILITARY KIDS!

Notes:

About the Author

Laura is a teacher with extensive experience working with children and families on U.S. military locations in the US and overseas. For 10 years she was a volunteer Navy Children's Story Time program creator and presenter. Throughout this time, she too was a military wife and mother. She continues to teach, write and sing, and owns 'Miss Laura's Music & Play, Inc.' located in Minnesota. She helps countless children and families successfully develop and grow in early childhood literacy, ESL, music & fitness.

Music & Play
Miss Laura

It is my pleasure to thank you for purchasing this set. It is certain that everyone will love the book, the activities, and the songs. They can even bring a tear to your eye. Make the most of each child's time. Don't forget to make memories that remind them of how special they are to hold the title of 'Military Brat'.

-Laura